After Your Deer is Down

After Your Deer is Down

The Care and Handling of Big Game

Joe Fischl
and
Leonard Lee Rue, III

Photos by Leonard Lee Rue, III

Winchester Press
Tulsa, Oklahoma

Library of Congress Cataloging in Publication Data

Fischl, Joe.
    After your deer is down.

    1. Game and game-birds, Dressing of. 2. Cookery
(Game) 3. Big game hunting. I. Rue, Leonard Lee.
II. Title.
SK283.8.F57   664'.90281   81-10335
ISBN 0-87691-353-2   AACR2

Published by Winchester Press
    1421 South Sheridan Road
    P. O. Box 1260
    Tulsa, Oklahoma 74101

Book design by Joy Flora
Printed in the United States of America
1 2 3 4 5 85 84 83 82 81

To my children, Kirk and Wayne

—Joe Fischl

To my deer-hunting buddies, Dan and Bumper Bacon, Rick Dotzenrod, and Charlie Angelini

—Leonard Lee Rue, III

Introduction

"Waste not, want not." That is a maxim that I was brought up on. It was a necessity for anyone brought up during the Depression. The validity of that statement is as true today as it was then, and it will again become a cornerstone for the future.

Being a farm boy, I was used to cutting up and preparing for the table the various types of livestock. Game was done the same way as a matter of course. Doing all of your own meat preparation was a matter of pride, and you knew that everything was done properly, under sanitary conditions, and the portions were just as you wanted them.

My methods of meat preparation have been published dozens of times in national magazines and books and have been followed by untold thousands of satisfied hunters. But we can always learn better ways to do things, and when I met Joe Fischl, I met a man with a better way. Joe is an artisan with a knife. A professional meatcutter, Joe was apprenticed in that trade in Germany at the age of 15. The methods that we will explain can be applied to most big game. They are the methods of a professional done so that the amateur can do the job properly, at a big savings in money, and with pride.

Leonard Lee Rue, III

Contents

Part 1

Photo Essay on the Care, Butchering, and Handling of Big Game

The deer after having been shot.

Roll the deer on its back, straddle the carcass, and hold it in this position with the back of your legs. Your first cut will be around the deer's rectum.

Insert your knife about 4 inches deep between the rectum and as close to the pelvic bone as possible. Cut around the rectum, pulling it aside as you cut to avoid cutting into it.

Insert the knife tip at the base of the breastbone. Pull up the skin and the flank with your other hand as you cut slowly with the tip of the knife so that the paunch and intestines are not punctured. Cut to within 4 inches of the testicles or the milk bag and stop.

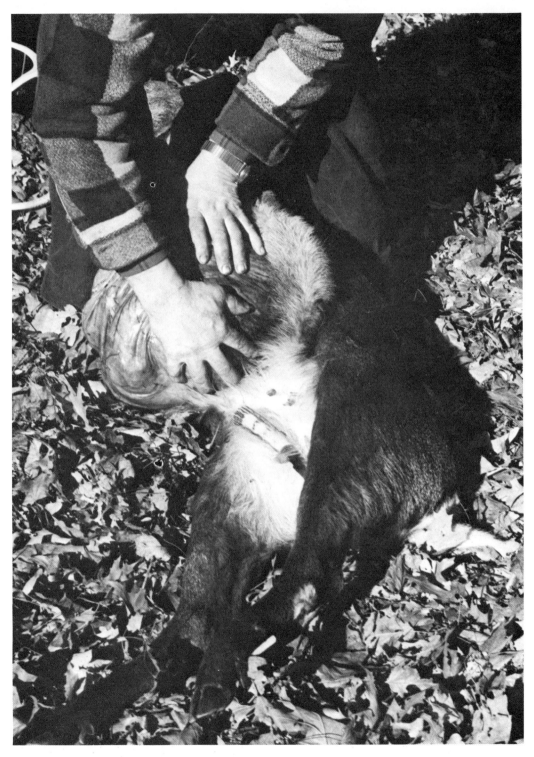

Roll out the stomach and the intestines. If you previously cut deep enough around the rectum, you should have no problem pulling through the rectum and the bladder.

Do not remove the kidneys and the kidney fat at this time because they will keep the fillets from getting dirty. The cut should not be longer than 12 inches. At this stage, the carcass is "field-dressed."

Cut around the diaphragm close to the rib cage. Then reach in and sever the windpipe as high up as possible.

Pull on the windpipe and, if needed, cut with your knife so that the liver, lungs, and heart come out in one piece attached to the windpipe. Now the carcass is "hog-dressed." Place the lungs, liver, and heart in a plastic bag (brought from home) to keep them from becoming soiled.

The cavity should not be larger than shown (12 inches). If you have cut into the paunch or the intestines, wash as soon as possible. If there is snow on the ground, use it to wipe out the cavity. If the cavity is very bloody, it should be washed out. Hang the carcass up by the head, hind legs down. When hung in this manner, all excess blood and water, if washed, will drain. Bloody residue causes meat spoilage.

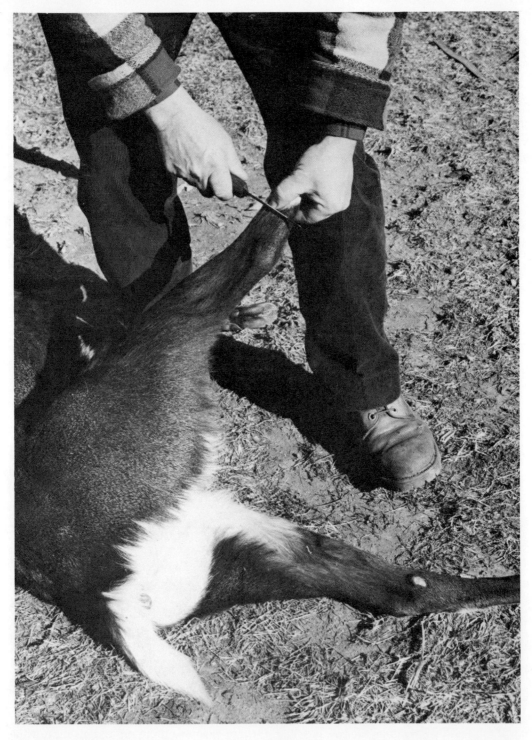

After the carcass has hung several days, it is ready to be skinned. Take it down and cut the hind leg at the joint. Do not sever the tendon above the joint because it is used to hang the carcass for skinning.

After cutting the skin around the joint, use your knee for leverage and break the joint. Repeat with the other hind leg. Then hang the carcass up by using gambrel hooks through the tendons above the joints.

Repeat the same cutting procedure on both front legs.

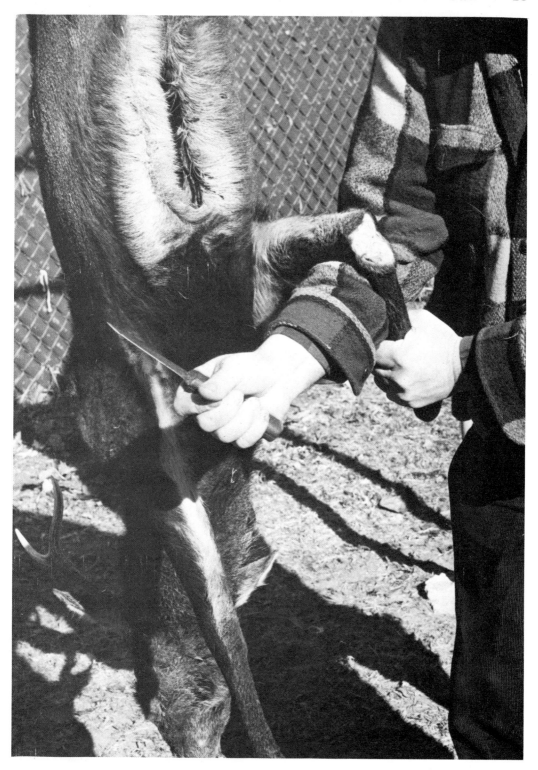

Use your right arm for leverage and break the joint with your left hand.

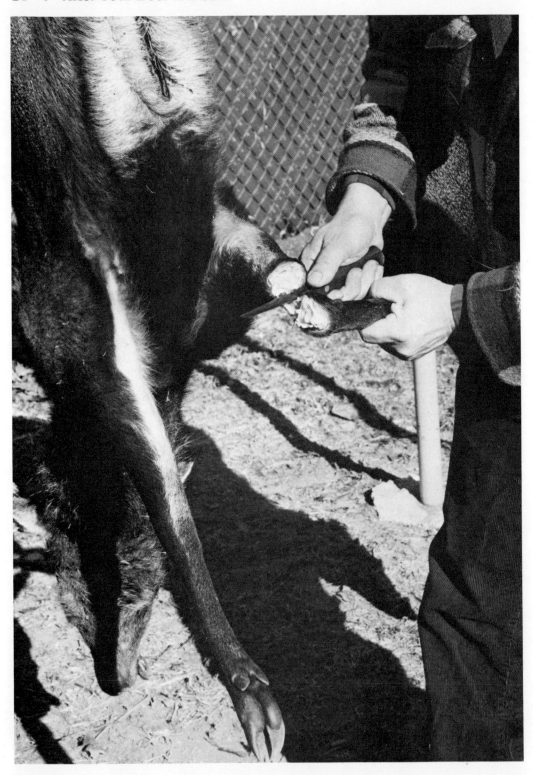

After the joint is broken, cut through remaining skin with your knife.

Method 1 is for skinning the deer when the cape is to be used for a shoulder mount for a trophy head. Start by slitting the skin at the end of the original abdominal cut up to the rectum cut.

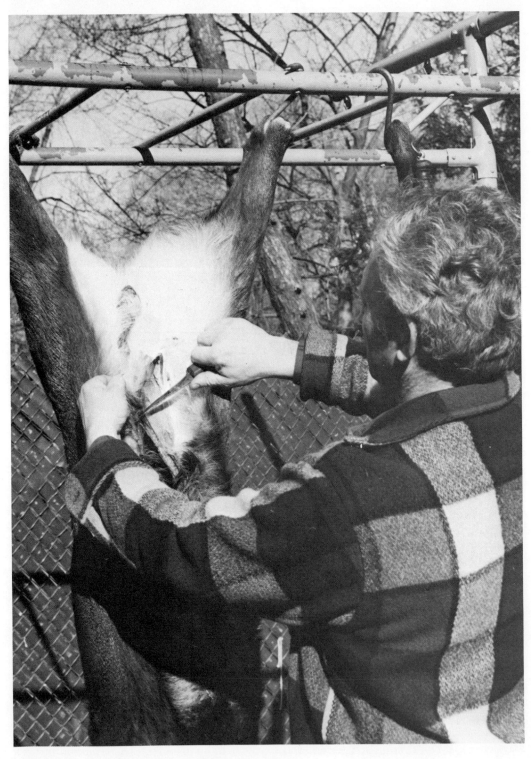

Start loosening the skin from the flank area.

Since this carcass is being skinned for a shoulder mount, make a cut 2 inches behind the shoulder. Cut all the way around the carcass making sure that you are definitely 2 inches behind the shoulder. Taxidermists require extra skin to make a good shoulder mount.

After completing the cut all the way around the carcass, cut the skin along the spine down to the head.

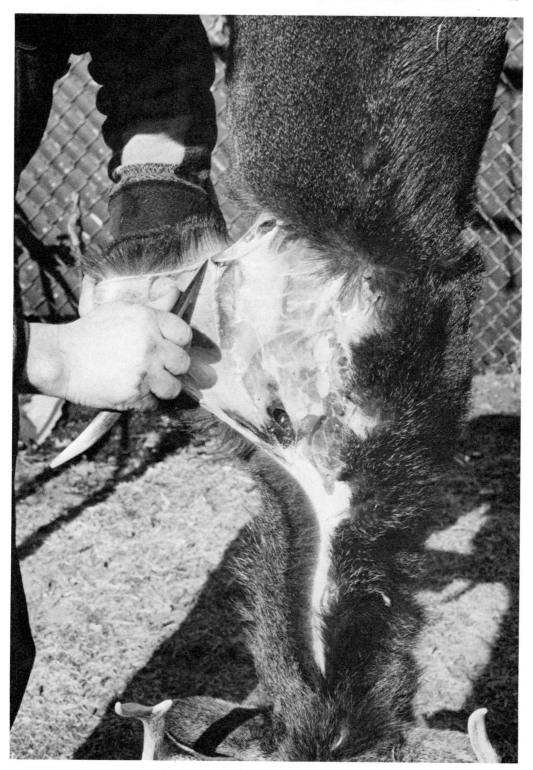

Use your knife to cut the skin from the shoulder.

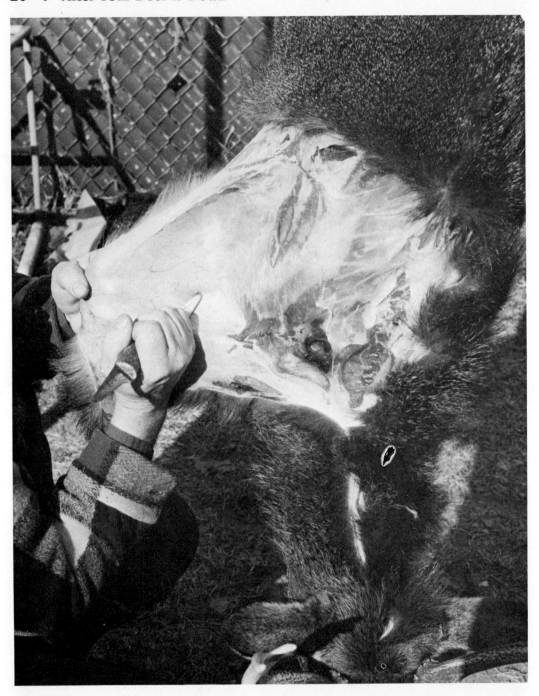

Hold the skin with your left hand and the special skinning knife, or an antler, with your right hand. Using the handle of the knife or the point of the antler, push and rip the skin with long up and down motions. Each stroke frees the skin in an area 1 foot long and 1 inch deep. The knife handle or the antler tip tears through the tissue holding the skin to the meat with no possibility of cutting the skin. Continue the up and down motion to free the skin.

Using the skinning knife, cut the skin of each leg from the joint to the cut behind the shoulder.

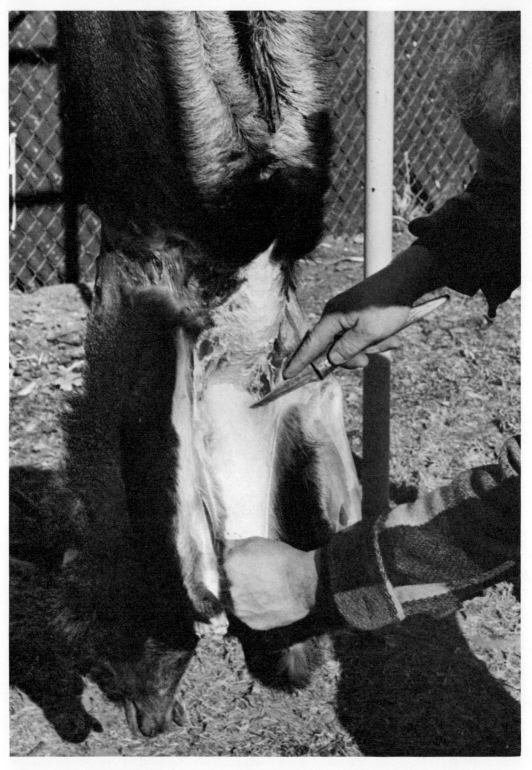

Skin out the brisket and the front legs. The skin is now ready to be pulled off.

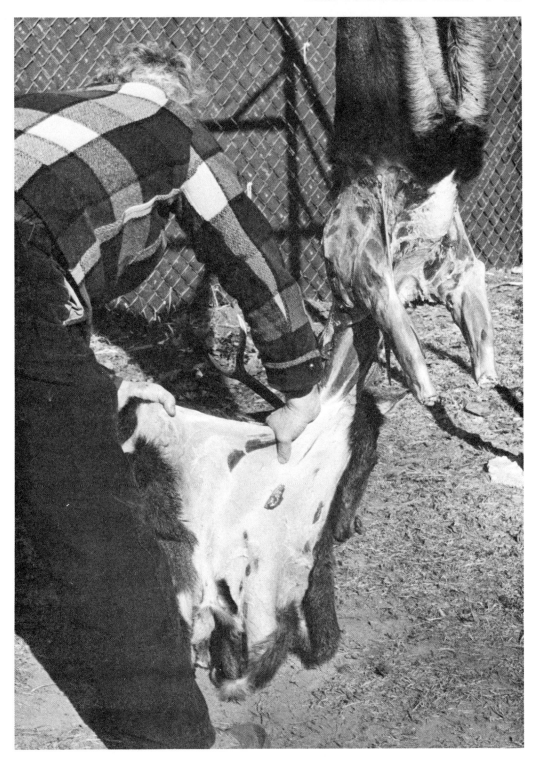

After making certain that the skin is loose around the front legs, remove the skin from the neck with a fast, strong, downward pull.

Cut through the meat and muscles all around the neck between the head and the first joint of the cervical vertebra.

Grasp the deer by the antlers or by the head and twist and the neck will break. Then cut through the remaining tendons, ligaments, and meat to completely sever the head.

Start to skin out the antlers by cutting through the skin to the base of the antler.

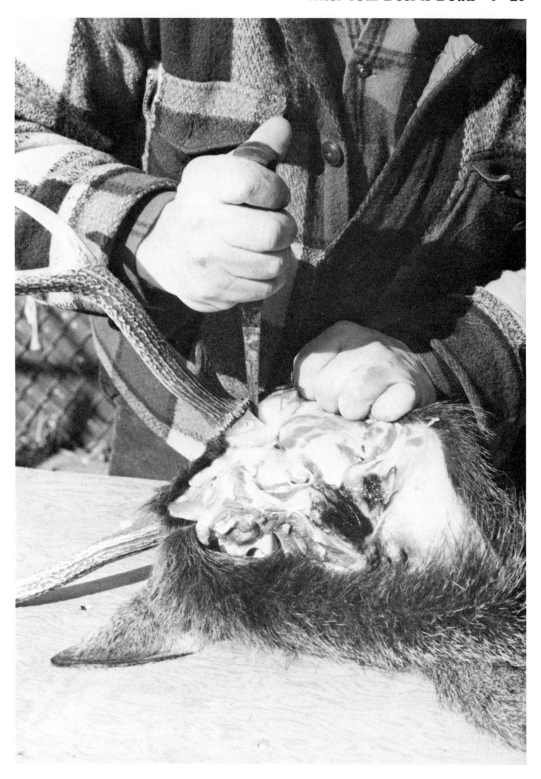

Cut around the back of each antler.

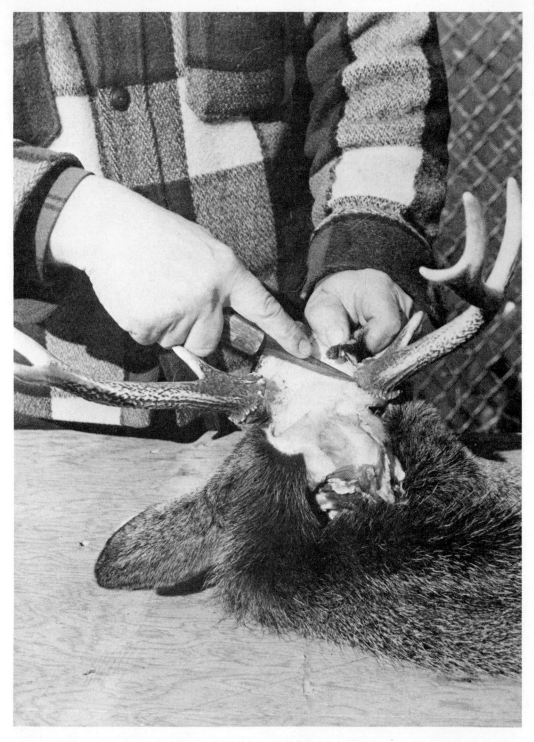

Cut the skin loose from the front of each antler. From this point on, great care must be taken not to cut through the skin anywhere on the face of the carcass because it is hard for the taxidermist to repair facial cuts.

Cut the skin loose from the forehead.

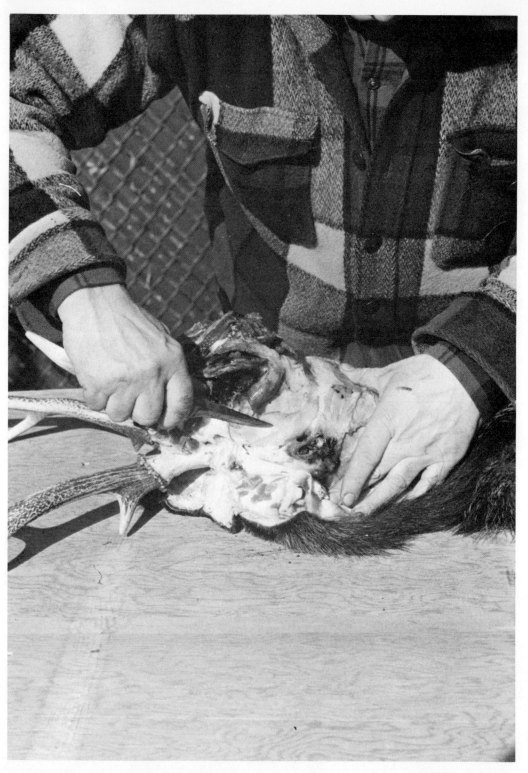

Cut the skin loose down toward the eye socket.

Carefully loosen the skin around the eye socket.

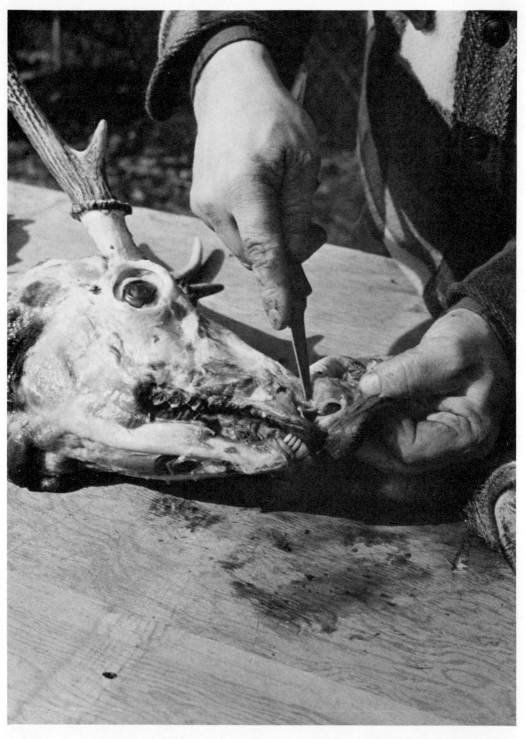

Continue to loosen the skin down toward the nose and along the jaws. Be careful not to cut into the teeth; they are the hardest bones in the deer and will ruin the knife's edge.

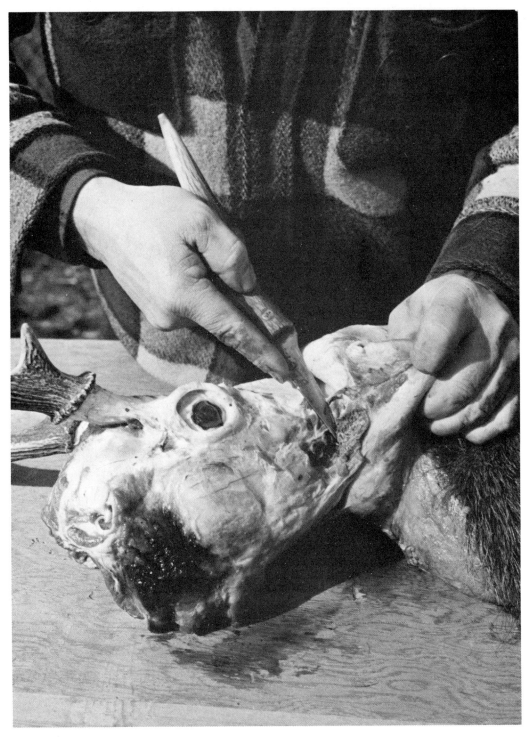

Be extremely careful when skinning out the nostrils and the lips because these areas cannot be patched or repaired by the taxidermist.

The cape and the skinned out head.

Saw through the skull across the eye sockets.

Saw down through the skull about 1 inch behind the antlers. The antlers and skull plate can now be separated from the rest of the skull. Every bit of meat must be removed from the antler base before it can be mounted by the taxidermist. The meat can be cut off or the base can be placed in water and boiled until the meat falls off.

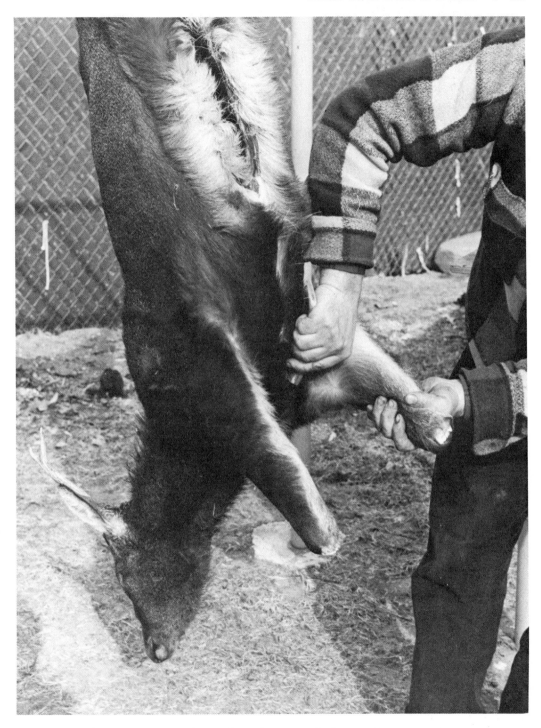

Method 2 is for skinning the deer when the entire hide is to be removed in one piece—when the neck skin is not to be used in the mounting of the head. Using the point of the knife, make a cut in the skin from the end of the rib cage, down over the brisket, and up the neck to the head.

Please note that in making any cut in the skin the knife point is inserted beneath the skin and the cut is made from the inside out. This will prevent the knife from being dulled on any dirt that is in the deer's hair and will prevent cutting the hair itself. Cut the skin on the inside of the leg from the end to the long vertical breast cut.

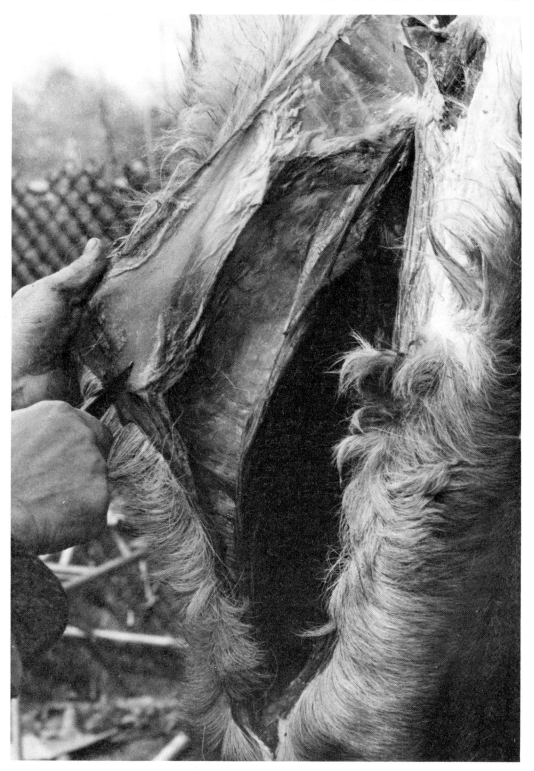

Cut the skin loose from the flank and belly.

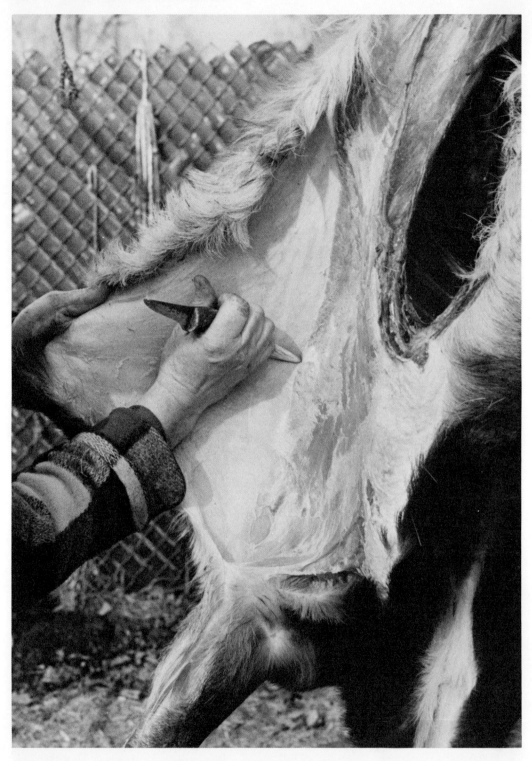

Using the special skinning knife or an antler tip, push and rip in foot-long strokes. Do it in this manner and you will not cut the skin or tear the meat.

Open the skin on the hind leg by making a cut from the rectal area along the top of the leg to the end. Then start to loosen the skin.

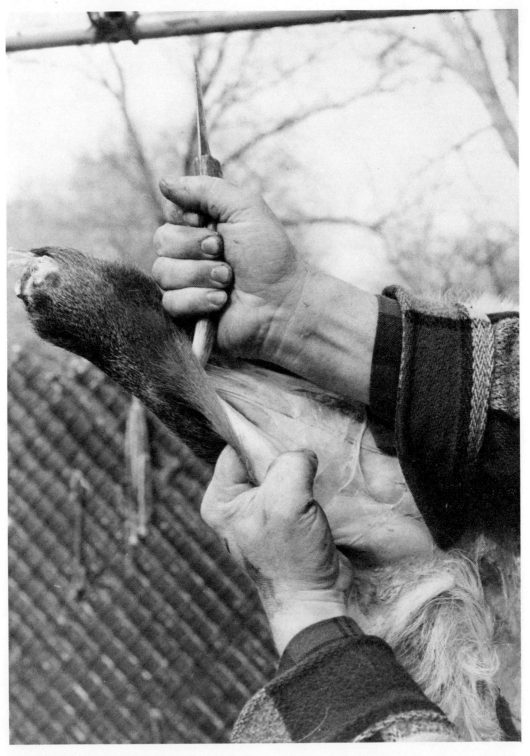

The proper way of holding the skin and the use of the special skinning knife or antler tip. The tip is pushed up against the tissue holding the skin on the carcass.

Unhook one hind leg from the gambrel hook. Hold the left hind leg with your right hand and pull the skin loose with your left hand.

Use the knife tip to cut the skin loose, making sure that the meat does not tear and that no meat is left on the skin.

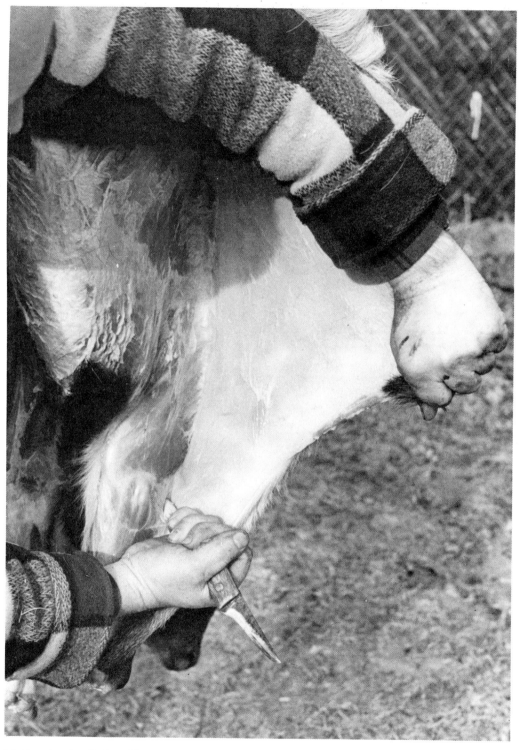

Using the knife handle or an antler tip, rip the tissues holding the skin to the body, removing the skin quickly and cleanly. Always hold the end of the skin tightly.

When skinning the hind legs, hold the skin with the left hand and put pressure on it with the right elbow and pull the skin downward. Always have the knife blade ready if the meat starts to tear.

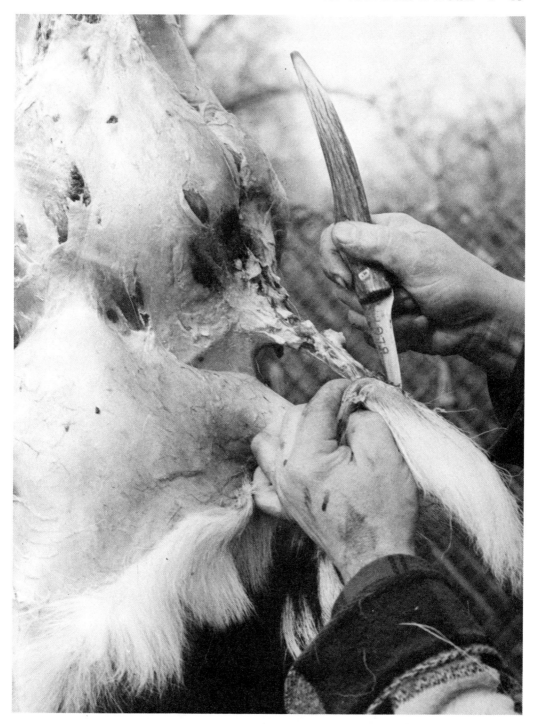

If the skin is to be used for leather, the tailbone can be severed close to the spine because that skin will not be tanned. Winter deer skins do not make good rugs because the hollow hairs break when walked on. If the skin is to be tanned with the hair on and used as a wall ornament, skin the tail.

Use your left hand to pull the skin up tight. Then proceed to rip the tissue loose with the back of the knife by pushing downward. At this stage, some fine meat fibers will adhere to the skin. These can be removed later.

Pull up on the skin with your left hand as you push the skin downward and loose with your right elbow.

Hold the skin upward with your left hand and push downward on the skin with the fist of your right hand.

You can also hold the skin upward with your left hand and loosen it by pushing down with your knee.

Remove the head by cutting around the neck between the skull and the first vertebra and break the neck by twisting it as described in Method 1.

Despite the greatest care, a few hairs will get on the meat. Use a small propane torch to singe off any hair from the carcass. After the skin and the head have been removed, the carcass is "city-dressed."

Cut off the forequarters between the fourth and fifth ribs. Note the small hand hook being used to hold the meat. This hook can be made easily if you can't purchase one.

On one side of the carcass, cut the loin strip across to the hip bone. This back is being prepared to cut out the loin strips.

Cut down the entire length of the loin on the sparerib side, staying 3 to 4 inches from the backbone.

Cut down the entire length of the backbone on both sides as close to the bone as possible.

After making the previous three cuts, hold the loin strip in one hand and cut it loose from the bone, cutting very close to the bone.

Repeat the previous four steps to remove the other loin.

After removing the loin from the carcass, place the loin on a table and pull the fascia off.

Remove all excess fat and tendon by careful trimming with your knife. We use a sheet of Plexiglas for a cutting board because it is more sanitary than wood.

An alternate method of cutting up the meat is used when the back is to be made into chops instead of loin strips. Cut cleanly through the meat to the backbone just in front of the hip bone.

With a handsaw, cut off the rib cage and the backbone from the legs.

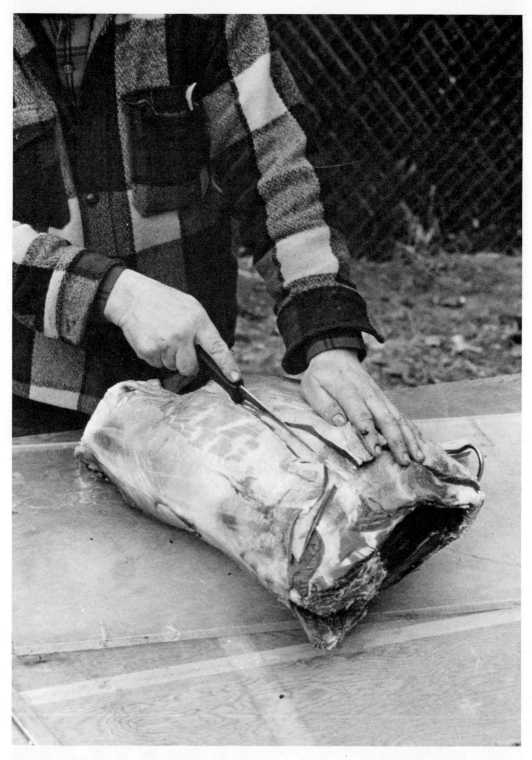

Put the back on a table and cut through to the ribs, about 6 to 7 inches from the backbone and parallel to it.

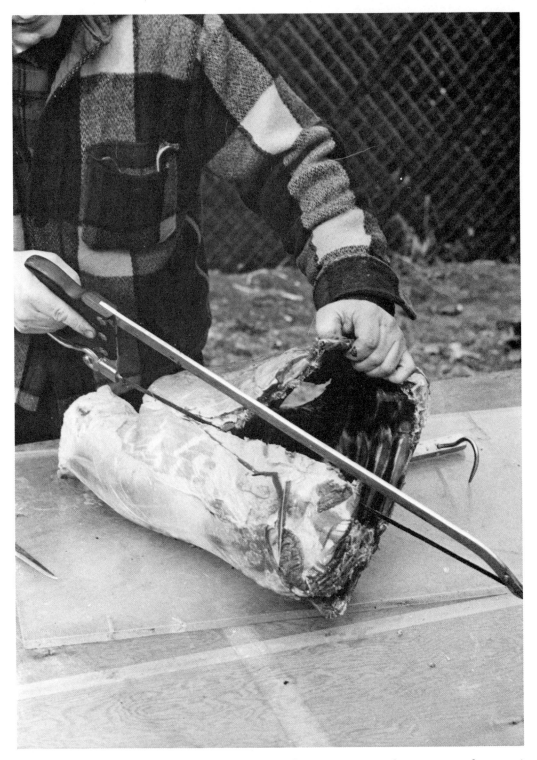

Cut through the ribs with a handsaw. Repeat the same cut on the opposite rib cage. A butcher's saw works best, but a carpenter's saw is satisfactory.

The spareribs removed from the back.

Remove the kidneys. Beneath the kidneys are two small fillets that must be removed only when you take out the loin strips. When making chops, as in this instance, leave the fillets in the back.

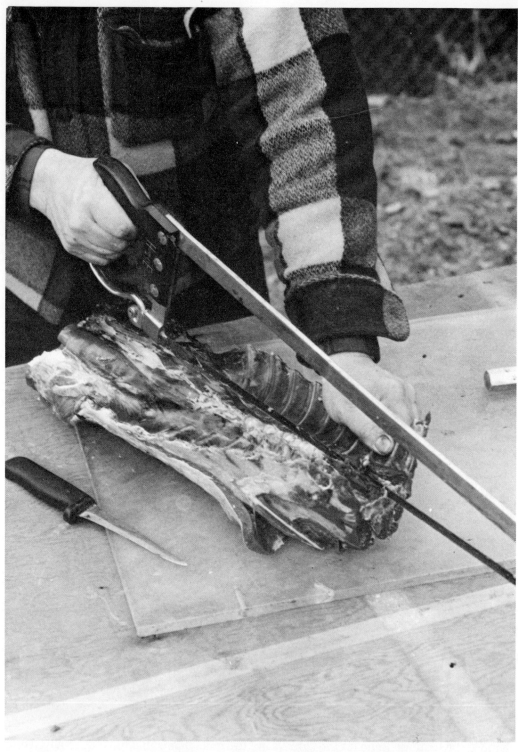

Saw directly down the middle of the back with a handsaw. This is done more easily if the back has been frozen for about 5 hours.

After the back is split, cut off the shoulder blade.

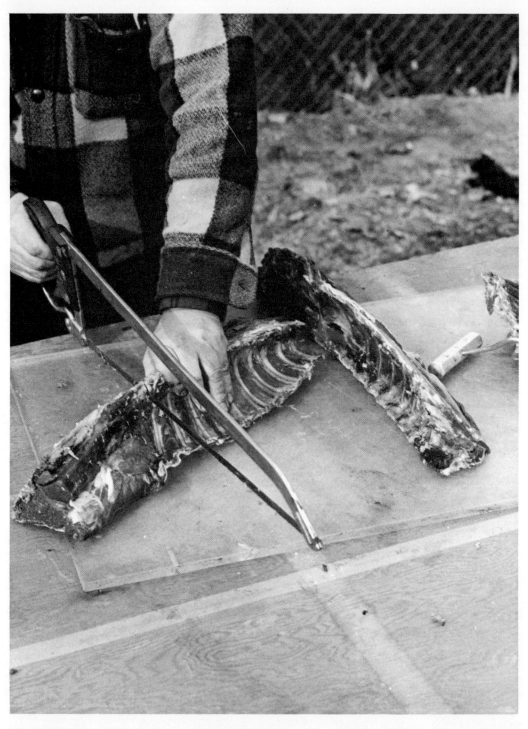

This back can now be used for either chops or a crown roast. In this photo, it is being prepared for a crown roast, for which only the rib portion is used. Cut the loin away from the rib end. When cutting the loin from the ribs, cut on the same angle that the ribs grow. The loin can be sliced and fixed as chops or it can be roasted.

Cut the backbone off the ribs.

Cut off the feather bone.

Cut off the meat from the top of the ribs. Cut off all loose meat and then cut next to the eye all across the ribs.

Cut out the meat between the ribs. Also cut out every other rib. To make a crown roast, bend into a circle and join the meat together using butcher twine or a butcher's needle.

A French crown roast, serving approximately eight people, ready for the oven.

Split the chest bone where the two sides of the spareribs are connected. On a young deer, this can be done with a knife.

On an older deer, the breastbone can be sawed or split with a cleaver.

Cut off the lower 2 inches of the breastbone so that the spareribs may be cut.

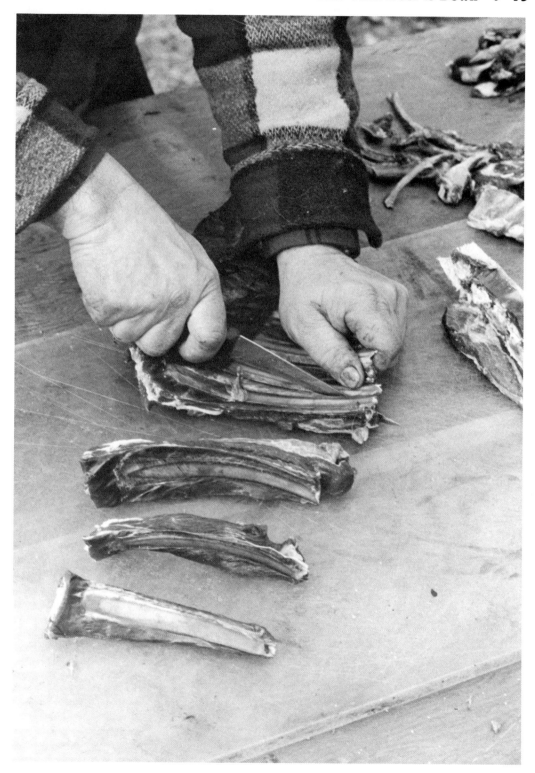

Cut each rib individually with a knife.

This back, which has been frozen for about 5 hours, is split through the middle with the handsaw, preparing it for chops.

Cut 1-inch chops with a handsaw.

Split a chuck, or forequarters, by cutting through the breast and up the throat.

Take out the windpipe.

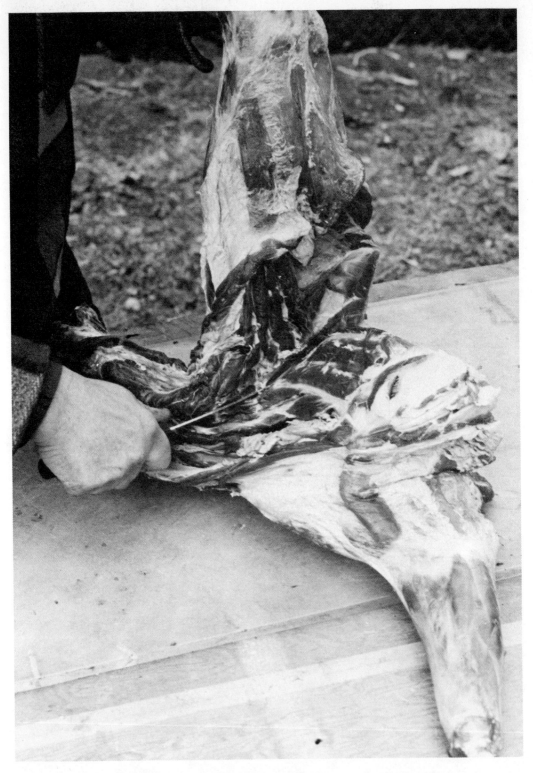

Bone out the chest and the neck, leaving the neck bone on the right side.

Bone out half of the neck and the chest bone (or chuck) on the left side of the carcass. Then bone out the right side of the neck and the chest.

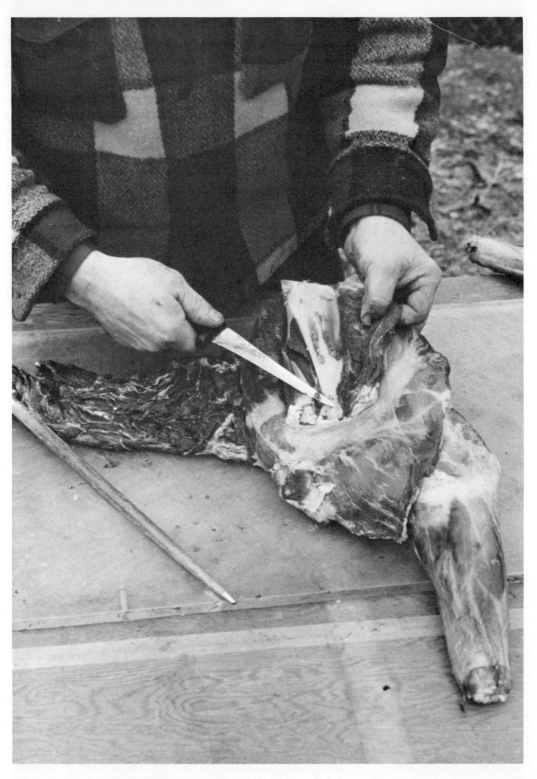

Bone out the shoulder blade.

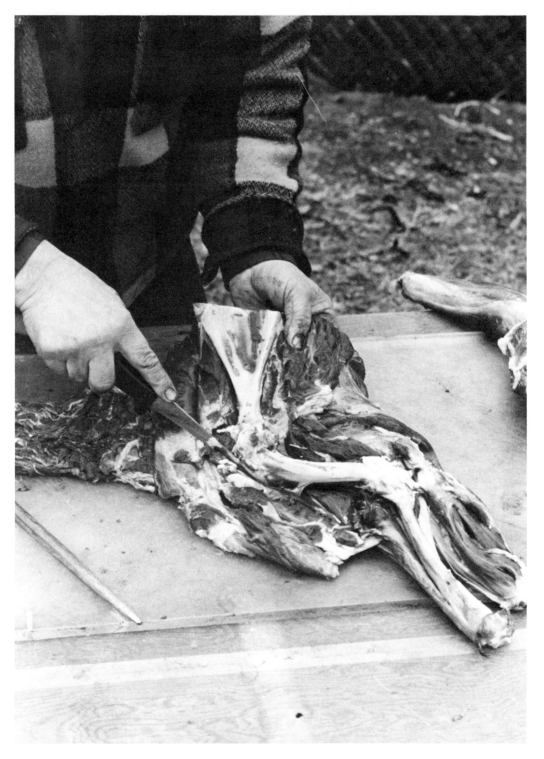

The bones of the front leg are visible, starting at the top: scapula (shoulder blade), humerus, and radius.

When boning chuck, hold the radius bone in one hand and cut around the humerus bone.

Hold the humerus bone with one hand while cutting around the scapula (shoulder blade) with the other.

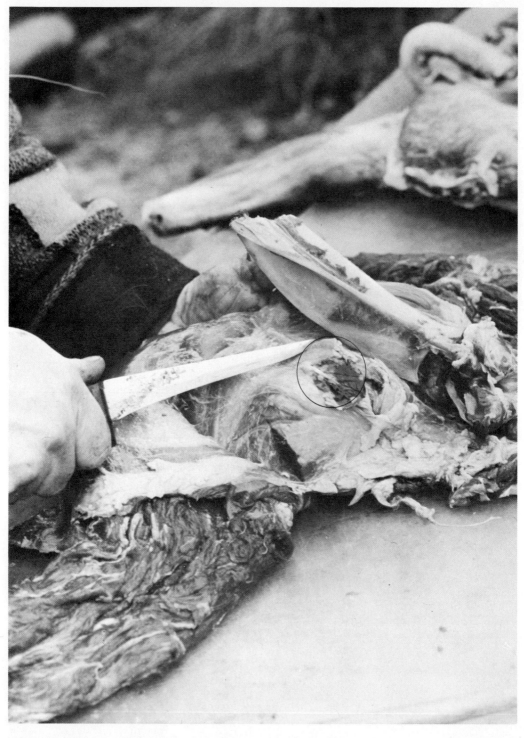

Under the scapula is the prescapular gland that must be removed before cooking because it will give the meat a bad odor. When the animal is in good condition, this gland will be buried in the fat and will not be visible without cutting into the fat.

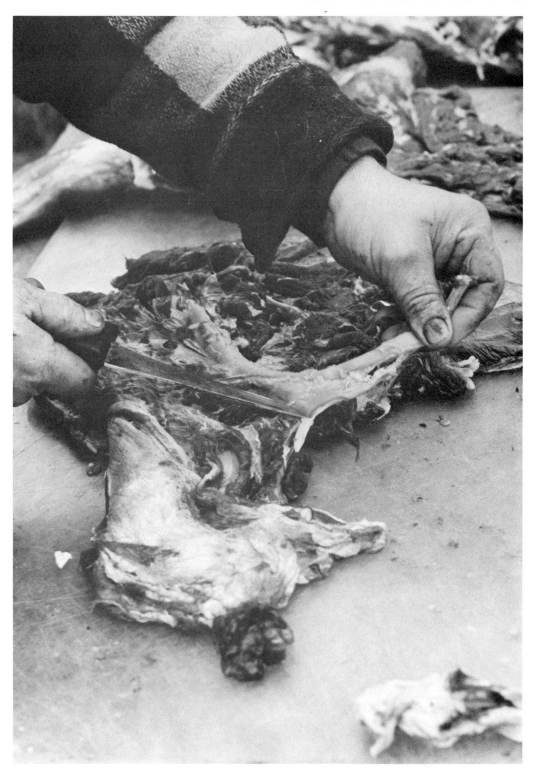

Take out the backstrap tendon from the chuck. It is located at the center of the neck.

Cut off the lower leg (shank) meat for stew.

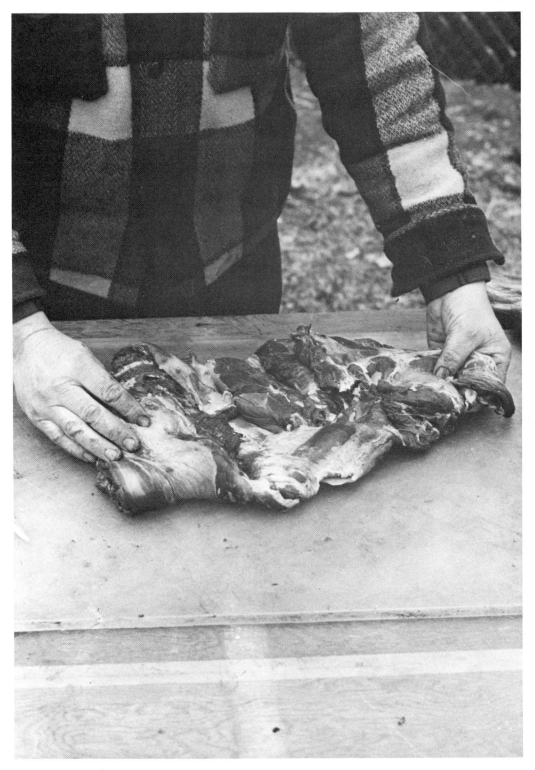

Check the meat and remove all excess fat. Then fold in the neck meat and chuck.

Roll the meat up, forming a roast.

Secure the rolled meat by using butcher twine.

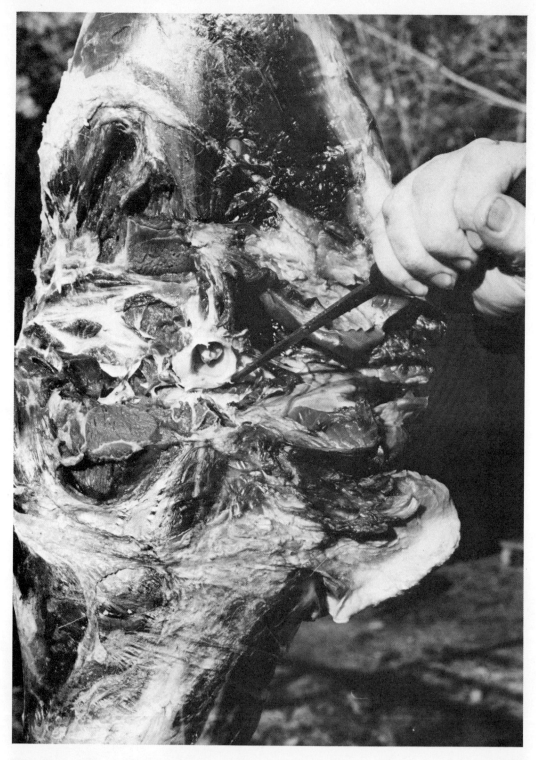

To start breaking down the hindquarters, remove the lower leg by cutting around the pelvic bone, severing the thighbone from its socket.

When boning out the pelvic bone, hold the knife very close to the bone to minimize meat wastage.

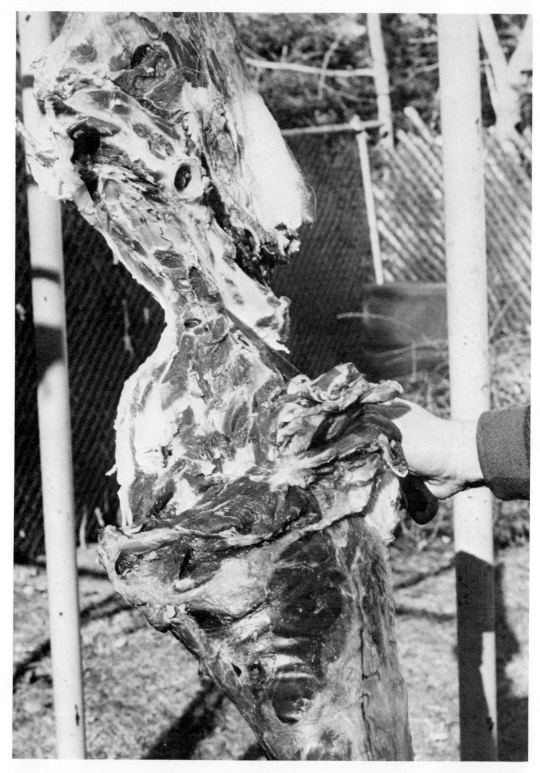

Sever the leg completely from the pelvic bone by cutting through the remaining meat.

The pelvic bone is severed from the femur of the other leg.

Completely remove the pelvic bone by cutting close to the bone.

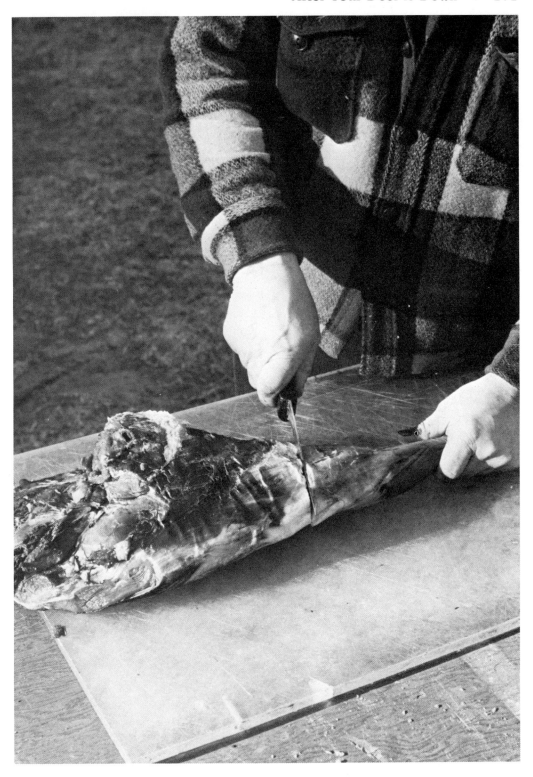

Cut off the shank portion of the hind leg at the joint.

Remove the popliteal (flank) gland from the fore part of the hind leg before cooking. If left in, it will give the meat an unpleasant odor and taste.

Trim all loose meat and excess fat from the hind leg, or ham. Place the ham in a plastic bag and freeze it for at least 5 hours, which will make the meat firm and easier to cut and slice neatly.

Use a handsaw to cut the thighbone in the frozen steaks.

The next procedure is how to break the ham down into the four major muscles, with the bone removed. Be sure to remove the flank gland.

The ham with the shank removed. Lay the ham with the thighbone socket up. Cut along the thighbone, which can easily be felt with the knife. Do not prefreeze the ham to cut it up in this method.

Split the ham lengthwise and remove the thighbone.

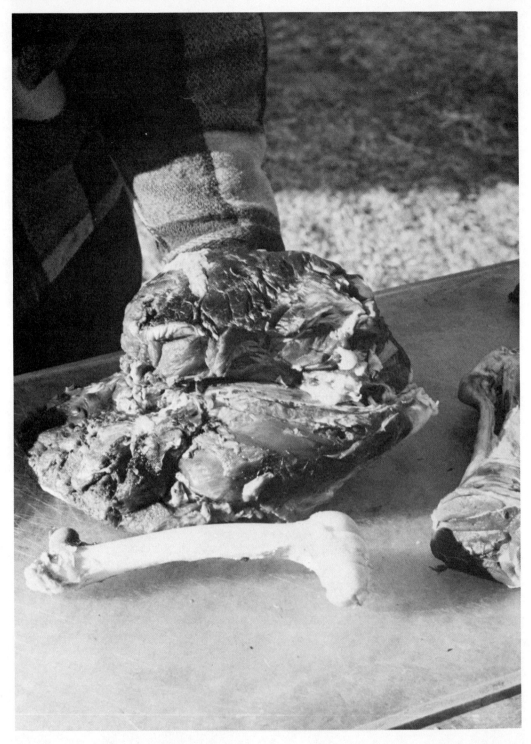

Remember to keep the knife tip close to the bone while cutting so that the bone is removed without meat being left on it. The bone should be clean and white, and there should be no deep cuts in the meat.

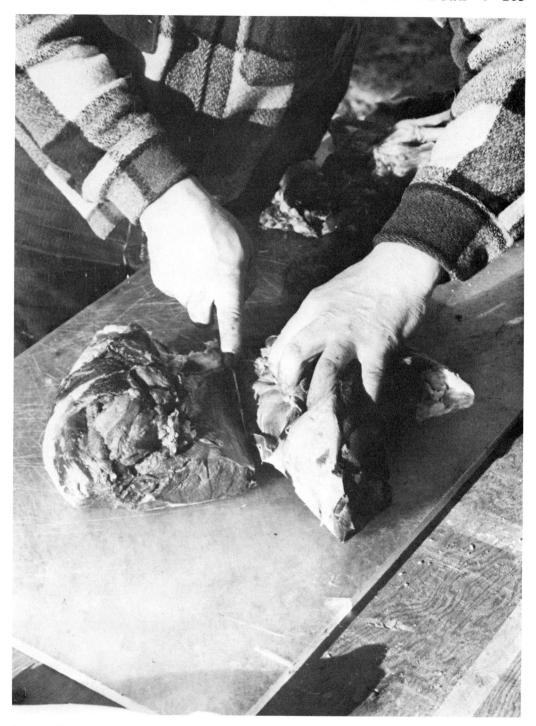

Cut the ham in half lengthwise between the bottom round and the rump roast. The meat just naturally separates between these two muscle masses. Leave the top round and the bottom round together making one roast of the two muscles. The top sirloin and the rump roast are also left together forming another roast.

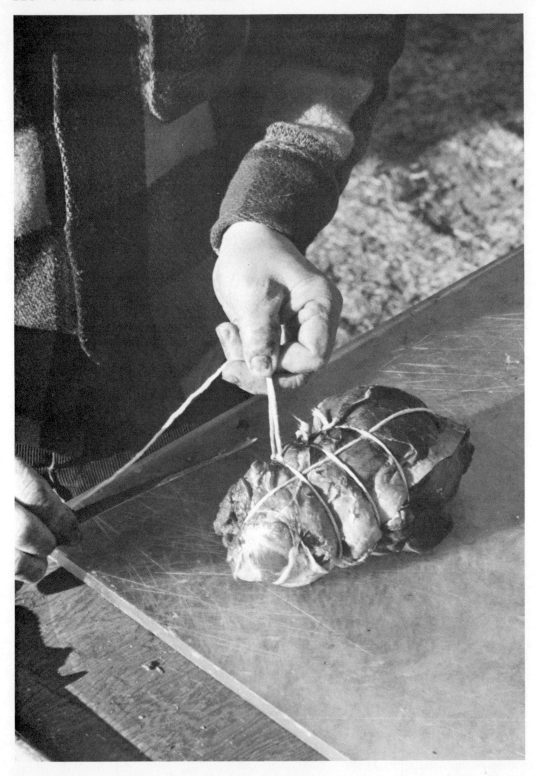

Tie the top sirloin and the rump roasts with butcher twine.

On the left is the top sirloin with the rump roast. On the right is the combination of the top and bottom round roasts. In the center is the shank with the bone still in it.

Bone out the shank meat.

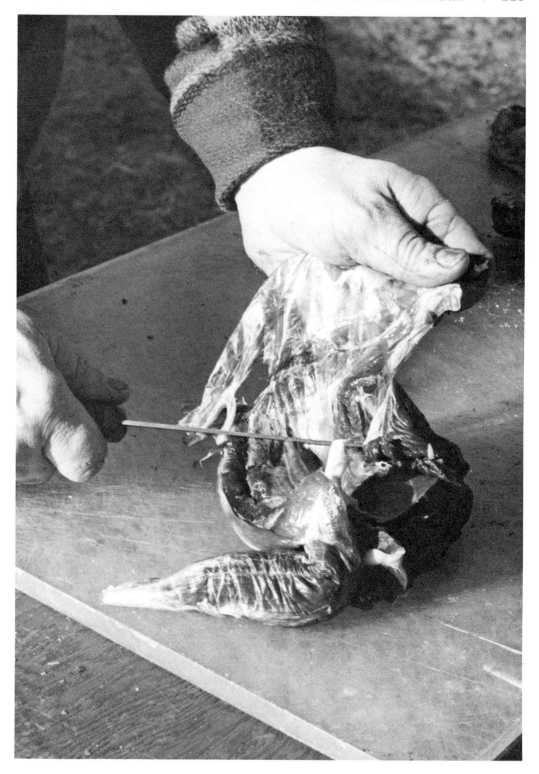

Remove the outer tissue and extra fat from the shank.

Cut the shank into long strips. Then cut the strips into 1-inch cubes for stew.

This is the entire carcass with the cuts identified from left to right, bottom to top. First row: spareribs and stew meat. Second row: chops and shoulder and neck roast. Third row: steaks from leg and the shoulder and neck roast.

The heart, liver, and lungs combined are called the "haslet." Here the heart is being separated from the lungs.

Cut the liver loose from the lungs. Deer do not have a gallbladder, as most animals do, so there is no danger of puncturing it.

Heavy butcher (freezer) paper should be used to wrap the meat for the freezer. The ends of the paper can be made air-tight by folding the seams over two times in what is known as the "drug store" wrap.

Then fold both ends in and hold in place with freezer tape or masking tape.

The complete deer carcass wrapped and ready to be put in the freezer. Each package of meat should be clearly marked. It is also a good idea to date the packages to show the age of the meat.

Out of the live weight of your deer, only a little more than one fourth is edible meat. For example, from a live deer weighing 127 pounds, only 35 to 45 pounds is edible meat.

Live weight of deer	127 pounds
Field-dressed deer	97 pounds
City-dressed deer	71 pounds

Head, feet, and skin	16 pounds
Haslet	10 pounds
Legs	27 pounds
Back	17 pounds
Chuck	22 pounds
Spareribs	5 pounds
	71 pounds

You have about 35 to 45 pounds of semiboned, edible meat. This is if your deer is shot in the right spot (4 inches after the shoulder or in the head if it is not a trophy). If it is shot in the chest, only a few spareribs will be ruined. If you shoot the deer in the neck or shoulder, you will lose a great deal of meat because all roasts are made from these areas. Never shoot a deer in the stomach or the rear end.

Deer meat cannot be aged like beef can because it is not fatty meat. If the temperature is 35° F. or 45° F. outside, you can leave an unskinned deer carcass hanging for about a week. If the temperature is warmer, the meat will spoil; if the temperature is colder, the meat will freeze. *Never* skin a deer carcass and let it hang. If skinned, it must be cut up the same day. Never cut out the tarsal scent glands in the field. When the deer is dead, all gland odors stop and the meat will not be affected. Also, do not remove the testicles in the field, minimizing field dressing and openings to keep clean and proving the sex of the deer.

Part 2

Selected Big Game Recipes

Recipes

Recipes provided by Joe Fischl

Fillet of Venison—Hunter Style

Venison:
4 thick fillets of venison, cut from the loin
salt and pepper to taste
1 medium-sized onion, peeled and sliced
2 small carrots, sliced
4 sprigs parsley
2 bay leaves, crumbled
½ tsp. thyme
pinch rosemary
⅔ cup dry white wine
1 capful white vinegar
½ cup olive oil
2 tbsps. sweet butter

Have fillets cut into steaks about ¾ inch thick. Season steaks generously with salt and pepper. Place in pan with onion, carrots, parsley, bay leaves, thyme, rosemary, wine, 6 tbsp. olive oil, and vinegar. Cover and refrigerate 24 to 48 hours (the longer the better to tenderize meat and remove gamey taste), turning fillets in marinade several times. To cook, remove venison from marinade, reserving marinade. Pat dry fillets. Heat remaining oil and butter together in large skillet. Cook fillets 3 minutes on each side—longer if preferred well done. Remove fillets to heated serving dish while preparing sauce. Make sauce in same cooking pan.

Sauce:
2 shallots, minced
3 tbsps. sweet butter
1 tbsp. flour
⅓ cup strained marinade
¾ cup dairy sour cream
salt and ground pepper to taste
few drops fresh lemon juice

Pour off excess fat from cooking pan in which venison was cooked. Sauté shallots in butter until soft. Sprinkle with flour and cook, stirring until mixture is lightly browned. Add strained marinade, sour cream, salt, pepper, and lemon juice. Serve at once over hot venison fillets. Apple sauce or red cabbage goes well with this dish.

Deer Stew—Ragú

shank or neck meat—1 lb. cut into ½-inch pieces
3 onions, minced
1 clove garlic, minced
1 green pepper, minced
3 tbsps. bacon fat
2 tsps. salt
1 tsp. sugar
¼ tsp. black pepper

Brown onion, green pepper, and garlic in bacon fat. Mix spices with meat and brown approximately 15 minutes. Pour in ½ cup water. About one-half hour later, add another ½ cup water. Let all ingredients simmer until meat is soft. Serve with potatoes and noodles.

Deer Chops

4 ¾-inch chops
½ tsp. salt
¼ tsp. pepper
¼ tsp. garlic salt
¼ tsp. MSG (Accent)
2 eggs
½ cup bread crumbs

Mix all spices and sprinkle on meat. Beat eggs. Dip chops into eggs and roll in bread crumbs. Brown in hot skillet. Place on separate pan after browning, cover with foil, and put in oven at 350° for 25 minutes. Serve with potatoes or wild rice.

Deer Burgers

1 lb. lean deer meat
1 onion, minced
2 eggs
3 tbsps. bread crumbs
5 slices bacon, minced very fine
1 tsp. salt
¼ tsp. pepper
¼ tsp. MSG (Accent)
1 tsp. mustard
1 tbsp. ketchup

Mix all ingredients thoroughly. Make six burgers. Fry in iron skillet. Serve with mashed potatoes or serve on buns.

Roulade of Venison

salt and pepper to taste
3 onions
3 tbsps. bacon fat
bacon strips
6 slices boneless deer steak

Slice boneless venison into ¼-inch thick slices. Flatten with mallet to tenderize meat. Lay flat pieces of steak on table and place one strip of bacon and a few slices of onion on each piece of meat. Roll up meat and fasten with toothpick. Salt and pepper roulade to taste. Preheat bacon fat and brown onions. Then add meat and brown. Add approximately 1 cup of water and cook meat till well done. Then mix 1 cup of water and some flour and use to thicken gravy.

Rack of Deer—French Style

7 or 8 ribs
1 tbsp. salt
1 tsp. pepper
1 onion, minced
2 cloves garlic
5 strips bacon
1 cup water

Season meat with salt and pepper. Add minced onion and garlic cloves. Lay bacon slices on top of ribs. Brown in oven at 400°. When browned, reduce heat to 350°. Add 1 cup water and let simmer for 1 hour. After meat is done, strain gravy and mix 1 or 2 tbsp. of flour with 1 cup of water and use to thicken gravy. Serve with wild rice or potatoes and vegetables of your choice.

Venison Sauerbraten or Pot Roast

4- or 5-lb. deer shoulder or neck roast
2 tbsps. salt
1 tsp. black pepper
1 tsp. paprika
2 bay leaves
1 tsp. peppercorns
1 tbsp. brown sugar
2 tbsps. wine vinegar
2 onions, minced
2 garlic cloves
1 quart water

Mix all ingredients except roast. Put roast into mixture. Marinade for 3 days, turning twice a day. After 3 days, drain marinade and strain it, reserving 1 cup. Do not discard onions, peppercorns, etc. Put these things into Dutch oven along with roast. Add 3 tablespoons bacon fat. Brown meat, then add reserved marinade, about 6 or 8 ginger snaps, and 2 cups of water and let simmer for 1½ hours, covered, until done. Remove meat and strain gravy. Serve with potatoes or rice, string beans, and carrots.

Deer Spareribs

1 side of deer ribs, cut between ribs
1 tbsp. salt
1 tsp. black pepper
1 cup olive oil
1 tsp. celery salt
1 tsp. garlic powder
2 tsps. paprika
1 onion, grated

Mix all ingredients and brush on spareribs. Let stand 1 day in mixture. Prepare on grill or broiler.

Deer Roast

4-lb. roast
1 tbsp. salt
1 tsp. paprika
1 tsp. black pepper
2 tbsps. bacon fat
3 onions, cut small
2 bay leaves
3 whole cloves

Season roast with salt, paprika, and black pepper. Place bacon fat in cooking pan along with onions, bay leaves, and cloves. Brown at 400° for about ½ hour. Heat 1 cup red wine with 1 tablespoon currant jelly. Soak 1 slice of pumpernickel for ½ hour in red wine mixture. Pour over roast. Turn oven down to 350°. After 1 hour, add ½ cup of water and let simmer till done. Serve with potatoes or rice.

Venison Boneless Loin or Boneless Leg Roast

3 to 4 lbs. of meat
1-cup butter, melted
1 tsp. black pepper
1 tbsp. salt
1 tsp. sugar
1 tsp. garlic salt
½ tsp. paprika
1 tsp. celery salt
1 beef bouillon cube, mashed

Cut meat into ⅛-inch thick strips. Mix all spices with melted butter. Preheat skillet. Dip meat into melted butter mixture. Fry 1 minute on each side. Then serve on hot garlic bread or French bread.

Deer Shish Kebab

    1 lb. meat—steaks
    1 cup olive oil
    1 tbsp. wine vinegar
    2 tsps. salt
    1 tsp. brown sugar
    1 tsp. celery salt
    1 tsp. paprika
    ½ tsp. black pepper
    2 cloves garlic, sliced

Cut steaks in ¾-inch cubes. Mix all ingredients and marinade meat for 3 days. Then place the following on shish kebob sticks:

    1 piece meat
    1 mushroom
    1 small onion
    1 pepper slice
    1 cube bacon
    1 cherry tomato

Repeat to fill stick. Place on grill until done. Serve with mashed potatoes and fresh corn.

Deer Steaks

    1-inch steak with all fat removed
    1 onion, minced
    1 tbsp. bacon fat
    salt and pepper to taste
    2 oz. tomato sauce

Using iron skillet, fry onion in bacon fat until golden brown. Place seasoned steak in skillet and brown. Pour in tomato sauce. Let simmer 30 minutes uncovered. Serve with potatoes and mixed vegetables.

Pepper Steak

    1 lb. deer steaks, 1-inch thick
    1 can mushrooms
    2 tbsps. bacon fat
    1 lb. onions, minced
    ½ lb. green peppers, minced
    salt and pepper to taste

Slice steak into strips 3 inches long and ⅛ inch thick. Put all ingredients into iron skillet. Fry until golden grown. Add meat and mushrooms. Simmer about 20 minutes, uncovered. Boil potatoes, carrots, and celery (cut small) in one pot. When done, drain, saving 1 cup of cooking water. Add to meat. Put in vegetables and mix together. Cover and let simmer for 5 to 7 minutes.

Deer Scallopini

1 lb. deer steaks cut into ⅛-inch thick slices

Pound pieces of deer meat with mallet. Salt and pepper to taste. Beat 2 eggs, adding small amount of milk. Place bread crumbs on a plate. Dip meat into egg mixture and roll in bread crumbs. Put 2 or 3 tablespoons of bacon fat into iron skillet and preheat. Place breaded meat in hot skillet and brown. Serve with mashed potatoes and asparagus spears.

Deer Liver

Fry six slices of bacon and one minced onion. When bacon is crisp and onion is brown, remove from skillet. Place deer liver into bacon fat and fry till done. Salt and pepper to taste.

Heart, Tongue, Kidneys, and Spleen

Marinade:
1 quart water
¼ cup wine vinegar
1 tsp. salt
1 tsp. brown sugar
1 onion, sliced
1 tsp. black pepper
1 tsp. paprika
2 cloves garlic, sliced
2 bay leaves
5 peppercorns

Mix marinade. Butterfly heart, kidneys, tongue, and spleen. Wash thoroughly and put into marinade, leave for 3 days. Boil all meats until meat is soft. Put meat into cold water until cold enough to slice. Before slicing anything, remove skin from tongue. Then slice all meats into shoestring slices. Strain marinade. Bring strained marinade to a boil in separate pot. Taste the marinade to make sure it is not too sour. If it is too sour, add water. Then take 3 tablespoons flour and brown it with butter in skillet until golden brown and mix with marinade. Put all sliced meat in gravy. Serve with potatoes or noodles.

Deer Rücken or Back of Deer

½ of back
1 pint of vinegar
1 pint of water
1 tsp. peppercorns
4 bay leaves
3 onions, sliced

Boil all ingredients for 10 minutes. Cool and pour solution over deer meat and let cool. Put into refrigerator for 2 days. Take meat out of solution and dry. Add 2 tablespoons butter to meat and put into 400° oven. Brown meat for ½ hour. Turn oven to 325° for 15 minutes. Pour 1 cup of solution over meat. Brown 2 tablespoons of flour and 1 tablespoon butter in skillet. Add 1 cup of water to browned flour and make gravy. Serve with potatoes and mixed vegetables.

Recipes provided by Charles Angelini, professional chef and mayor of Roseto, Pennsylvania

Venison Scallopini

From small pieces of venison, have butcher prepare miniature cutlets to desired amount. In large skillet, sauté oil or shortening, diced onions, garlic (not powder), and chopped parsley. When slightly browned, remove from pan (add more shortening if necessary) and place cutlets (previously dipped in beaten egg and seasoned flour) in this pan to brown lightly on both sides. Pour sautéed onion mixture into pan with cutlets, removing any undesired fat. Add tomato sauce to cover. Cook 30 to 45 minutes. Just before serving, add 1 cup sherry or burgundy wine. Cover and heat to simmer. Turn off burner and let set 5 minutes, then serve.

Venison Liver

If you like liver, you will find this a sumptuous repast. Have your butcher cut liver from ½ to ¾ inch thick. Dip pieces in seasoned flour and fry in greased pan, turning liver when blood begins to ooze. Cook to desired doneness. Delicious for breakfast with pancakes, fried eggs, or onions.

Venison Heart

Venison heart is delicious pickled in a mixture of ¾ vinegar and ¼ water (or to desired strength) combined with pickling spices and sliced onion. To prepare heart for pickling, cut in half lengthwise. Wash thoroughly, put in pot, cover with water, add onion, celery, and bay leaf, and boil. Cook approximately 30 minutes or until tender. Skim occasionally while boiling. When done, remove from water, cool, and slice. Season with salt and pepper, cover with pickling liquid. Refrigerate for use.

Venison Kidney

What a pity the kidneys of deer are seldom used! First, remove the membrane and then wash and slice the kidney. Fry slices in a greased pan with salt, pepper, and garlic. When almost done, add button mushrooms and sherry, burgundy wine, or tomato sauce.

Spareribs of Venison

Even though the rib cage may show more blood than desired, do not discard. Have the butcher cut ribs for sparerib portions. Refrigerate and soak overnight in saltwater. The next day they will look as appetizing as any you may see in a meat showcase. Cook according to your favorite sparerib recipe. My way of preparing is to use a shallow baking pan and sprinkle well with barbecue sauce.

Venison Cutlet

Have your butcher prepare cutlets. Dip cutlets in beaten egg, then in seasoned flour. Fry in cooking oil until almost done. Remove from pan and drain. Place slices of mozzarella cheese over cutlets. Pour hot spaghetti sauce into baking pan, place cutlets in this, and add a little sauce on top. Bake in 350° oven until cheese is melted and lightly brown. Serve immediately.

Roast Venison

Have your butcher prepare venison for roasting—leg, loin, shoulder, or neck. Have as much fat as possible removed and have it boned if you prefer. Pour olive oil into palm of hand and rub entire roast with this. With knife point, slit roast in several places and insert cloves of garlic—not powder. Season with salt and pepper and dust with flour. Cover top of roast with bacon strips. Place roast in cooking bag (sitting in a pan) and add celery tops, small peeled carrots, parsley, quartered onion, and cored apple halves and fasten bag according to directions on bag. Set oven temperature at 400° and place roast in at once. When bacon begins to sizzle, lower oven temperature to 350° and cook until done. Baste occasionally during cooking time, if open pan is used. Make gravy from drippings and serve with wild rice or other vegetables as desired.

Roast Venison

    1 venison roast—7 to 11 lbs.
    pepper and salt to taste
    1 large apple, peeled and sliced
    1 package dry onion soup mix
    Worcestershire sauce
    ¾ cup water
    barbecue sauce, if desired

The roast must be lean. Season the meat, place in a roasting pan, and cover with apple slices. Make a paste with onion soup mix and water. Spread the mixture over the roast and apple slices. Sprinkle Worcestershire sauce over meat and add ¾ cup water. Cover and cook at 250° for approximately 5 to 7 hours. Add some water to keep the roast from sticking to the pan. When the roast is done, discard all pan liquid. Top with barbecue sauce (optional). Serves 14 to 18.

Venison Jerky

    any lean cut of venison
    salt
    pepper
    Liquid Smoke

Cut the meat into 6-inch strips, ½ inch wide and ¼ inch thick, with grain running lengthwise. Trim all fat from the meat, season it, and brush it with Liquid Smoke. Place a round toothpick through one end of each strip of meat. Line the oven with aluminum foil to catch all drippings. Suspend meat strips from the top oven rack, with the toothpicks holding the strips in place. Cook at 120° for approximately 8 hours, until the meat is dark and dry. While the meat is cooking, leave the door of the oven slightly ajar so that moisture can escape. Strips are ready when they are thoroughly dry and bend without breaking. Keep the meat strips in a sealable plastic bag.

Venison Stew in Crockpot

1 to 3 lbs. venison stew meat
5 carrots, sliced thin
3 potatoes, sliced thin
1 apple, chopped
1½ tsps. salt
¼ tsp. thyme
3 tsps. instant minced onion
1 cup apple cider

Put the carrots, potatoes, and chopped apple in Crockpot. Add the meat and sprinkle with salt, thyme, and minced onion. Cook 10 to 12 hours on low heat. Thicken gravy to consistency desired.

Barbecued Venison

venison roast
¾ cup vinegar
1¾ cups water
salt
pepper
garlic to taste
4 strips bacon
Italian salad dressing or barbecue sauce

Place the venison in a big container and cover it with water and vinegar. Leave in marinade at least 4 hours, turning several times. Remove the meat and wash it thoroughly with cold water. Put garlic pieces into slits in meat. Lay the bacon strips on top of the roast. Add salt and pepper and cook 4 hours over low charcoal, basting with barbecue sauce or salad dressing.

Venison Meatball Appetizer

1 lb. ground venison
milk
¼ cup bread crumbs
1 medium onion, minced
salt and pepper to taste
1 egg, slightly beaten
2 tbsps. parsley, chopped
2 tbsps. cheese, grated (Romano, Parmesan, or your choice)

Soak bread crumbs in milk, then drain. Mix all ingredients in bowl, then shape into about 50 bite-sized meatballs and flour lightly. Melt butter or olive oil in a skillet and brown meatballs. Remove meatballs and stir 1 15-ounce can of tomato sauce into the skillet. Heat, then add meatballs, and simmer 10 minutes, stirring occasionally.

Venison Sauerbraten

1 venison roast, approximately 2 lbs.
6 peppercorns
5 whole cloves
3 bay leaves
1 cup red wine
water
3 tbsps. fat
6 carrots, cut in half
6 small white onions
1 cup celery, cut into ¼-inch pieces
1 tbsp. sugar
10 gingersnaps, crushed

Trim all outside fat from the meat. Put the roast into a deep glass dish. Combine pepper-corns, cloves, bay leaves, and wine. Pour over the meat. Add water to cover. Cover the dish and refrigerate for at least 2 days, turning the roast at least twice a day. Remove the meat from the dish and reserve marinade. Brown the meat on both sides in a Dutch oven or a cast-iron pot. Add the vegetables and 2 cups of marinade. Slowly simmer until the meat and vegetables are done, approximately 1½ to 2 hours. Remove vegetables and meat from the pot, leaving the marinade. Add sugar and gingersnaps to the marinade to make gravy. Slice meat thinly and serve with vegetables and gravy. Serves 4.

Venison Stroganoff

1 lb. venison, cubed
flour
¼ cup butter
1 clove garlic
½ cup onion, chopped
1 tbsp. salt
⅛ tsp. pepper
1¼ cups water
1 cup mushrooms
1 cup sour cream

Roll venison cubes in flour and brown in butter with garlic. Add salt, pepper, and chopped onions. Cook approximately 3 to 4 minutes. Stir in water and simmer 30 minutes until tender. Add mushrooms and sour cream and heat, but do not boil. Can be served over rice, noodles, or mashed potatoes. Serves 4.

Stuffed Venison Steaks

2 to 3 lbs. venison round steak
¼ tsp. meat tenderizer
2 cups dry bread crumbs
4 tbsps. celery, chopped
¾ cup onions, chopped
½ tsp. salt
⅛ tsp. pepper
⅛ tsp. poultry seasoning
⅛ tsp. sage (or to taste)
2 tbsps. butter or margarine, melted
water
2 cans (6 oz). tomato sauce
2 tbsps. bottled taco sauce

Trim fat from steaks. Sprinkle steaks with meat tenderizer, pound with a meat mallet, and set aside. Melt butter in a pan and sauté celery and onion until tender. Place bread crumbs in a bowl with the butter mixture, seasonings, and enough water so that mixture is sticky. Place 2 to 3 tsps. of mixture on each steak, roll, and secure with toothpicks. Steaks should not be too big. Brown steaks in greased skillet. Mix tomato sauce and taco sauce according to taste and pour over browned meat. Simmer slowly for 1 hour or bake at 350° for 1¼ hours. Serves 6.

Venison Allagash

Hindquarter of venison (small)
1 cup burgundy wine
1 tbsp. parsley, minced
1 can mushrooms, reserve liquid
2 green peppers, chopped
1 onion, chopped
4 cloves garlic
2 sticks butter or margarine
3 strips lean bacon
1 tbsp. flour

With a sharp knife, cut a pocket by the leg bone from the large end almost to the small end. Fill pocket with the chopped vegetables except parsley and mushrooms. Season the roast well inside pocket and rub well outside. Pour wine over roast and let set about 20 minutes. Cook in covered roasting pan for 3 to 4 hours at 350°. When done, remove meat from pan, add flour and juice from mushrooms, and mix well. Add parsley and mushrooms. As gravy thickens, cook 5 minutes. For a successful dinner, put roast back into gravy and cook, uncovered, for 5 minutes or until brown. Slice and serve.

Roast Venison Vinaigrette

2 to 3 lbs. venison roast, cooked
1 cup oil
1 cup vinegar
1 tsp. prepared mustard
1 garlic clove
1 tsp. salt
¼ tsp. pepper
1 onion, sliced

Slice cold, cooked roast into small pieces. Mix remaining ingredients except onion. Alternate layers of roast and onion in a casserole dish and top with seasoning mixture. Refrigerate for 24 hours, stirring occasionally. Serve.

Texas Deer Chops

6 venison chops, ¾ inch thick
1 onion, finely chopped
tarragon vinegar
dash Tabasco sauce
1 tsp. hot mustard
dash Worcestershire sauce
chili sauce
½ cup bourbon whiskey

Simmer chops and onion, covered with ¼ inch of tarragon vinegar, in an iron skillet until chops are very tender. Add the rest of the ingredients and stir until the mixture is thick. Cook on low heat, stirring when necessary, and add more vinegar or chili sauce if needed. When sauce is thickened, spread both sides of chops generously and place in a shallow pan. Pour bourbon over them. Bake, uncovered, at 350° for 1½ hours, basting occasionally. Serves 3.

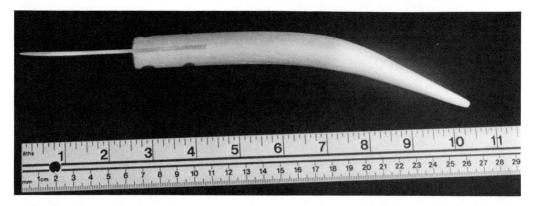

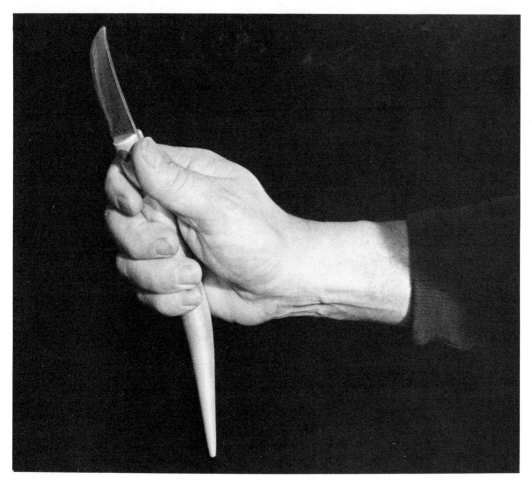

The skinning knife used in this book was designed by Josef Fischl. This handmade knife is a professional tool, built to accommodate both the beginner and the experienced skinner. Its hand-fitting contour and skillfully designed blade make skinning faster and easier than the job is with a conventional knife. For further information or to order a knife, write to Josef Fischl Enterprises, 362 Westwood Avenue, Westwood, NJ 07675. Be sure to include your return address.

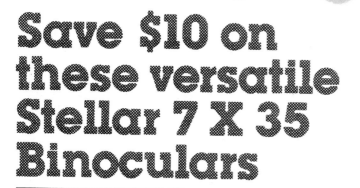